THE WILD LIFE
in an
ISLAND HOUSE

GAIL KARLSSON

Illustrations and cover by Gail Karlsson
Layout and design by Jonathan Gullery

Published by:
Virgin Islands House
P.O. Box 1522
Cruz Bay, St. John
U.S. Virgin Islands 00831

Disclaimer:
This book is not an authoritative nature guide and
has not been reviewed or endorsed by anyone with
any scientific training. Nevertheless, it might contain
some interesting information for people who come to
the Caribbean looking for paradise and wonder why
there are so many bugs and things here.

"The more clearly we can focus
our attention on the wonders and realities
of the universe about us, the less taste
we will have for destruction."
—Rachel Carson

Contents

Introduction

*I*N 1990, MY HUSBAND AND I WERE living in lower Manhattan and spending almost all of our time working. I was a lawyer at a Wall Street firm and my husband was a computer programmer. He drove to Long Island every day, leaving at six in the morning, and was often not home until 9 pm. I had reduced my work schedule after having a baby, but still was gone until 7 pm ('half-day' they joked at the firm) and had a full-time German nanny to look after my two year old son.

That January we decided to take a 'time-out' vacation in the Virgin Islands and for three weeks rented a house overlooking Cruz Bay in St. John. We took our son and the nanny, and invited some friends and relatives to come down as well. We had such a great time that my husband almost immediately began to formulate a plan for doing his computer programming long distance so he could live and work in 'paradise'.

After much planning and negotiation, in the fall of 1990 we rented a house in Fish Bay, on the south shore of St. John, for six months. After the initial excitement of the move, I began to feel that Fish Bay was a bit too far out in the bush for me. Before long I wondered how I had gone so quickly from being an overworked Manhattan lawyer to barefoot, and pregnant again, in the islands.

Towards the end of the six months rental period I was more than ready to go back to New York. My husband, however, was already laying down roots. When the opportunity came up to buy a small house next to the place we were renting, it seemed like a good investment and a way to make sure we could come back whenever we wanted.

Since 1991, we have lived off and on in our island house, going back and forth between St. John and New York. Learning to get things done on island time provided a sharp contrast with Manhattan, which is actually an island about the same size, but which requires a whole different set of survival skills.

For me, the greatest attraction of living in the Caribbean, besides the amazing beauty of the surroundings, is the feeling of being part of the natural world. That was something I missed out on when I was growing up in New York, where almost all of the land was covered with concrete and the wildlife I saw was limited to roaches, pigeons, and occasional squirrels in the park. But summers at my mother's family house on the coast of Maine took me into spruce woods and blueberry fields and the wildness of cold Atlantic water along rocky beaches. Those memories of outdoor freedom kept drawing me back to the Maine coast for summer vacations, and also fueled my long-term interest in environmental law and conservation. Then when my husband and I went to the Caribbean for our honeymoon, we discovered the joys of beaches located in warmer climates.

Many of my Manhattan friends have been envious of our island retreat. Running away and living in a tropical paradise is a powerful fantasy, especially during dismal northern winters. My friends have sometimes been amused by my stories about living in the bush, or sympathetic to tales of flying debris, but they generally still imagine island life as lying around on the beach all day with a rum punch and a trashy novel.

I have certainly spent plenty of lovely days at wild beaches, and have felt myself blessed to have that opportunity. Yet at other times I have found island life altogether too challenging, in part due to our physical isolation and vulnerability to threatening storms. And given the limitations to my own self-sufficiency, I have never really been comfortable in the role of 'pioneer mom'. As our small island has become more 'civilized', however, I have become concerned about the loss of some of its essential wildness.

Over the years, although I have explored many coral reefs and hiking trails, some of my most interesting nature studies have been focused on the small companions I have found in and around my own house. Many of them are bugs of one sort or another, some of which, like the mosquitoes, everyone is familiar with, and some of which have probably never been identified or documented. My first impulse was to go to war with them, but over time I have come to know a few of them quite closely and have learned to respect many of them, even if I don't really love them. Besides the bugs, large and small, other visitors or inhabitants in and around the house have included birds, bats, rats, lizards, scorpions, toxic frogs and stray cats – a veritable witch's brew.

Our interactions with these household partners have helped define my family's life in the islands. Despite their sometimes unwelcome intrusions, I have found that living alongside these other life forms and observing their intricate behaviors and inter-actions has given me a greater understanding of the long history of life on this planet and a deeper appreciation of the complexity and mystery of my own relatively brief time on earth.

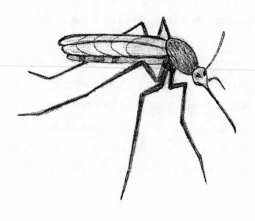

Mosquitoes

*A*LTHOUGH THERE ARE MOSQUITOES almost everywhere, at least during the summer months, the climate in the Caribbean is warm enough to support a lively mosquito population all year round. Most people can't think of anything good to say about mosquitoes, and I'm not going to be the one to try to convince you that they can teach you profound lessons about the meaning of life while they are buzzing around your ears or biting your ankles. Their most important role seems to involve providing a plentiful food source for a lot of other creatures, some (but not all) of which are more pleasant to have around.

Historically, one of their major accomplishments was to keep down the numbers of people living in the tropics. The Europeans who 'discovered' the Caribbean brought smallpox and typhus, and Africans later added yellow fever and malaria to the mix. The native Taino people had no immunity to these diseases, which contributed to their rapid disappearance from the smaller islands. In addition, few Europeans were able to survive the epidemics of yellow fever or malaria they encountered in the islands, although they did not realize that these diseases were transmitted by mosquitoes. So many Europeans died horrible deaths soon after arriving in the Caribbean colonies that it became impossible to get wage laborers or indentured servants, or anyone with a choice in the matter, to work there. Many West Africans, however, brought to the Caribbean against their will to work on the sugar plantations, had been exposed to malaria and yellow fever and had some degree of immunity to it.

The fact that the mosquitoes in the Caribbean don't currently carry malaria is thanks to copious spraying of DDT in the 1950s and 60s, when it was still viewed as a new miracle compound. At that time malaria was widespread in the southern states of the

US, as well as throughout Europe, Asia and the Caribbean, and killed millions of people every year. Yellow fever had been easier to control earlier when people learned that it was caused by a virus transmitted by the Aedes aegypti mosquito. This type of mosquito lives near people and can't fly very far. Covering cisterns and water containers to prevent mosquitoes from breeding in them helped limit the recurring outbreaks of the fever as it was reintroduced to crowded port cities by new arrivals.

Malaria is spread by the female Anopheles mosquito, which is more common in rural areas than in towns. When a mosquito bites an infected person, or anyone who once had malaria, it picks up microscopic parasites in that person's blood and passes them along to the next person it bites. Systematically spraying DDT all over an island can kill most of the mosquitoes and thereby keep the disease from spreading. Even though the mosquitoes come back, if no one has the disease, the mosquitoes can't pass it around.

In 1962, Rachel Carson wrote the famous book, Silent Spring, that spurred the beginning of the environmental protection movement. It turned out that DDT wasn't just killing mosquitoes. Its effects were so toxic and long-lasting that it was killing birds and fish and beneficial insects as well. By 1970, the US stopped widespread spraying for mosquito control, but a number of countries where malaria is pervasive and deadly still use DDT because they have not found effective substitutes.

When we first moved into our house, people told us to pour bleach into the large cistern that catches the rain running off our roof (our only source of water) to get rid of the mosquitoes, and anything else that might be living in there. That didn't sound healthy to me, but when it appeared that Cuban toxic frogs had moved into the cistern, I decided a little chlorine probably wouldn't hurt us.

Unfortunately, many chemicals used to kill 'pests' have turned out to have disastrous long-term health and environmental impacts. There is a new United Nations treaty to phase out the use of DDT, along with other pesticides and toxic chemicals that have spread around the world in the air and water without decomposing. These chemicals can accumulate in the fatty tissues of animals and humans, causing cancer, infertility, and genetic mutations. It would be better if there were more testing and analysis before potentially dangerous chemicals become widely used. I guess it's sort of like throwing the bleach in the cistern, though. We don't know what it might do to us in the long run, but we'll do almost anything to get rid of the mosquitoes.

If there is stagnant water lying around after it rains (mosquitoes don't breed in salty water), the mosquitoes will lay eggs in even the smallest puddle or container. Within about four days the eggs will begin hatching. Besides making sure there is no place for mosquitoes to breed, the best thing is to try to keep the mosquitoes out of the house. Unfortunately, our screens have never been very effective, due to cats' claws, rat holes and inattentive people trying to walk through them. Some mosquitoes always sneak in, and most of the time we just keep the doors to the deck open. When it is rainy, and the otherwise steady trade winds die down in September and October, the mosquitoes sometimes seem to take over, and we have to retreat behind closed doors. Still, strong fans usually keep the bugs away while we are sleeping, and lots of other creatures keep busy during the night hunting them down.

Scorpions

WE MOVED INTO OUR ISLAND HOUSE full-time for a couple of years when my second son was a baby. The first night we all slept in one bedroom because work on the downstairs addition was not finished and most of the space upstairs was filled with boxes of furniture and fixtures shipped down from Florida. There was a double bed in the middle of the bedroom and on one side there was just enough space for a single bed mattress for my older son. On the other side we set up a portable crib for the baby.

I had brought mosquito nets that had come in handy during a summer trip to Maine, but there was no way to hang them over the beds. At least I was able to drape one of them over the crib to protect the baby in hopes he would sleep through the night without waking up and crying. We were all pretty tired from the trip and didn't wake up until sunrise when the birds started calling to each other.

When I got up and went to get the baby, I saw a large scorpion sitting on top of the netting, right over my son. I had seen a couple of these earlier during our six months in the rental house, but never so close and still alive. My husband had squashed one on the wall over our bed in that house, which left me with a very uneasy feeling about finding one in the bed with me. I don't know why that scorpion happened to come out and get onto the net above the baby. Scorpions come out at night to eat insects, and maybe his smelly little body was attracting some interesting bugs. Maybe the scorpion meant no harm, but my protective mother instincts were quickly aroused. I didn't squash it though. I didn't want to get that close to it. Instead I picked up the net and shook the scorpion out off the deck and into the bush below.

People said the scorpions here were not the kind that could kill you with just one sting, unless of course you happened to be allergic to them. Still we were advised to always check our shoes before putting our feet in them because scorpions like to crawl into dark damp places and don't like to be disturbed.

I never have found a scorpion in my shoe, and I definitely have checked, especially shoes that have been sitting in the back of the closet for a while. Years later I did get stung by one when I went to pick up a rock at the side of the road. It was a very sharp, shooting pain and I went back to the house as quickly as I could because I felt like my whole body might go into shock. Later I learned that the stingers have two toxin-producing glands, which is why they deliver such a shocking pain. Fortunately, the pain passed pretty quickly without any lingering effects. People who are allergic to bee stings, however, might have a worse time of it.

After doing some research, I found that the scorpions here are Bhutid scorpions. I also learned that scorpions were among the earliest land animals, dating back about 400 million years. Since they like to eat mosquitoes, I guess that means mosquitoes have been around for quite a long time too. It seems that we humans are just recent interlopers in an age-old drama involving stagnant water, breeding mosquitoes and ancient pred-ator-prey relations.

One day I found an apparently intact scorpion body just lying on the floor. I put it up on the counter with some other inter-esting found objects until I noticed that the tiny ants had discovered it so it was starting to look more like one of the hairy scorpions. I slid it into a small plastic bag and put it in the freezer for safekeeping. Later that week, we found another smaller one, and popped that one in as well.

Later I learned that my scorpion bodies were only the outer exoskeletons, or cuticles, shed by living scorpions as they grew. Like lobsters they have to shed in order to expand and grow. Apparently there is a hatch that opens up, starting around the mouth and side of the head. The hatch lifts up around the head area and the scorpion then pushes and crawls its way out. A new hard cuticle forms underneath and that helps loosen up and push away the old one. Sometimes a leg might not make it through the process and the scorpion has to grow a new one, but otherwise the shape of the old exoskeleton exactly matches that of the body.

I read that scorpions might shed up to seven times before they reach maturity. Some shed according to the seasons, but the Bhutid scorpions here seem to shed depending on how much they have been getting to eat. If the big one in the freezer was just a shell, I hoped the live scorpion wasn't still in the house somewhere getting super-sized on all the mosquitoes.

I also found out that mother scorpions give birth to live babies rather than laying eggs. They then carry the babies on their backs for a couple of weeks, until the babies shed the first time. After that they are supposed to be big enough to go out on their own. (One interesting fact is that if food is scarce, the mothers will sometimes eat their own offspring – evidence that children should not assume that maternal instincts will always lead to self-sacrifice.)

One of the most intriguing things about scorpions is that they are fluorescent, so they will glow under a black light. It is the outside cuticle that is fluorescent, and after the scorpions shed it takes a couple of days for the new one to develop the glow. The fluorescence may be caused by calcium salts stored in the cuticle. One source I came across suggested that rays from the moon bounce off the scorpions at night making them glow a bright blue/green, and attracting insects. Though all this would be invisible to the naked human eye, it is not hard to imagine scorpions setting out on a luminous full moon hunting party.

Spiders

*F*EW PEOPLE LIKE SPIDERS, PROBABLY because so many of them are poisonous. The good thing is that most of them have fangs that are too small to bite through human skin.

The hairy tarantulas here, however, (less threateningly referred to as 'ground spiders') certainly look big enough to deliver a nasty bite, though I have been assured that their venom is not deadly to humans. Mostly they hunt for insects on the ground at night. They are pretty shy and don't come into the house, unless the doorway opens out onto flat ground and they can just wander in. When we were renting the house overlooking Cruz Bay, our two year old son and the nanny were sleeping downstairs, and one evening

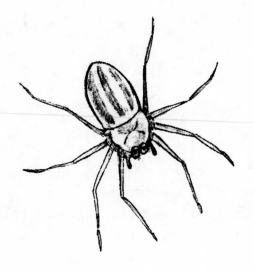

she called to me in terror because there was a big hairy spider on the floor halfway between the door and his crib. I had never seen anything like it before, but felt the need to take charge of the situation so I got a broom, stepped up briskly, and swept it back out into the garden. Later I heard that if they feel threatened, the tarantulas can use one of their legs to rub hairs off their abdomens and send them flying into the air to irritate the mucous membranes of would-be attackers. Fortunately I didn't learn about that from first-hand experience.

Most of the spiders around my house seem to be common cobweb spiders, or cellar spiders that look like daddy-long-legs. They don't seem very dangerous, and reportedly cobweb spiders can catch up to 1000 insects a night. Although that's good for mosquito control, I don't really like having cobwebs all over the place.

Some of the spiders live in the upper corners of the low-ceilinged rooms downstairs, which are still high enough that it is hard to reach them with the vacuum cleaner. The spiders hang around up there and seem to collect small packages of wrapped-up bugs (for later), though probably some of the pack-

ages are really egg cocoons. When I do get
around to vacuuming, I feel like a powerful
angry god sucking the poor spiders into a
whirlwind tunnel of death. Maybe there is
even an afterlife for some inside the vacuum
cleaner bag. I am always afraid they will get
out and seek revenge, so I am careful to wrap
up the bag and take it to the dumpster right
away.

The longer-legged spiders seem to prefer
the downstairs bathroom. When the bathroom light gets left on at night, it attracts an
amazing number of little moths and random
bugs that somehow sneak in through the
cracks. The spiders feed on them during the
night and then hide in the medicine cabinet
during the day. I hate it when I reach in for
my eyeliner and find a big-legged spider
hanging upside down right over my make-
up case. Usually when I open the cabinet
door they run away and hide further back
under the shelf, but it is a small space and
hard to avoid each other. It is also hard to get
the spiders out of there without taking out
all the little containers and supplies and
getting the vacuum. Then, before you know
it, they are back, so I have ended up getting
used to sharing the bathroom with them, and

just keeping a wary eye on them.

Like scorpions, spiders are arachnids, not insects, and they too shed their skins as they grow. Spiders have 8 legs, rather than 6 like an insect, and 6 to 8 eyes instead of only two. The ones in the house don't make elaborate webs, just irregular tangles of silk. They spin the silk by excreting a protein from glands in their abdomens. (Before there were Band Aids in the medicine cabinet, people used cobwebs as bandages because they help stop the bleeding.)

The spiders with webs don't hunt for prey. They just wait for an insect to come by and get tangled up in the web. Once the insect is trapped, the spider rushes over and injects it with venom. Cobweb weavers and cellar spiders have weak jaws so they can't chew up their prey. Instead they inject digestive juices into the insect's body and then suck up the liquefied internal tissue, leaving the exoskeleton intact.

There are other spiders, like the tarantulas, that don't make webs. They hunt down their prey and have more powerful jaws. Occasionally we will see a flat, round reddish-colored spider around the house. One of our neighbors reported that she got a nasty bite from one of those, so we call them the 'biting spiders'. I think they are a type of crab spider, a hunter that lies in wait to ambush its prey and can run sideways, like a crab. Some types hold up their front legs like claws to grab prey, though I have never seen ours do that. At night, going down the outside staircase, I try to remember not to grab onto the railing since sometimes one of those spiders will be sitting out there.

Lizards

*L*IZARDS ARE A PLEASURE TO HAVE in the house because they like to eat mosquitoes and other bugs but are not creepy like scorpions and spiders. It is especially gratifying to sit at dinner on the deck and see a lizard eating up the bugs that are attracted to the outside light. They sit around and wait for their prey to come near, and then quickly lunge at them.

The small lizards that come in the house are mostly a type of crested anole found only in the Virgin Islands and a couple of other nearby islands. There are over a hundred types of anole lizards in the Caribbean especially adapted to the different islands. Interestingly, from a Darwinian perspective, as the anoles living on different islands have

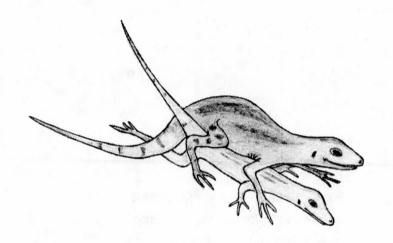

adapted to their environments, they have independently developed similar body shapes and relationships to their habitat, even though they are only distantly related genetically. The crested anoles usually live in trees, but some stay up on the top, some live only on the trunk, and others go back and forth between the tree trunk and the ground. I think those last ones are the ones most likely to come inside. On the deck there are sometimes smaller greener lizards that I think may be green anoles, but it is somewhat confusing. Like chameleons, some of these lizards seem to be able to change their color.

The lizards are very territorial, so when they come inside they tend to stick to one area of the house, and can come to seem as friendly and familiar as pets, unless you have a cat in the house, in which case the lizards are likely to lose their tails or, sadly, their lives, if they are not fast enough. (Rumor has it that wild cats who eat too many lizards will develop cataracts, though I have not been able to confirm that.)

The male and female lizards look so different that for a long time I thought they were different types of lizards. The females are small and generally grayish green with yellowish stripes down their backs. The males are larger and darker, more brown, and have sail-like crests along their tails. When they spread out the fan-like dewlap under their necks and do push-ups with their front legs, they look like miniature dinosaurs. They are intending to be intimidating when they act like that. The males are very aggressive about defending their territory from encroachments by other males, and if their display and posturing isn't enough to establish dominance, they might chase each other around and fight. Apparently this is most common in October when it is mating season and testosterone levels are high. There might be several females within one male's territory, which is why you are likely to see more of the smaller lizards.

At beach camp one summer, my sons learned how to dig in the sand at the base of a tree and find little white lizard eggs. They brought some of the eggs home in a cup and we actually saw a couple of them hatch, though they seemed very fragile and unfortunately didn't live very long. There was also an older boy who had a lizard he wore on his ear. Apparently he got it to bite onto his earlobe and it would hang there for quite a long time like a pirate earring.

I never experimented myself with getting a lizard to bite onto my ear, that being the sort of thing that appeals mostly to ten year old boys. I did once catch a lizard on a bet, though.

It was the very first time I came to St. John, during the period before we had children, when my husband and I were still investigating different islands. We were staying at Maho Bay Camp for Thanksgiving weekend, and were waiting in line by the pavilion to collect our turkey dinner. Some smart-aleck boy ahead of me in line said he had caught a lizard and bet me a dollar I couldn't do it. We had just discovered that my husband's wallet was still back in New York, and we had just enough money left in mine to pay for Thanksgiving dinner.

I figured I could use the dollar to buy a soda. Lizards can move very quickly, but after some patient watching and a quick fake, I was able to sneak my other hand around the tree and grab a little lizard when he jumped. After I let him go again, I collected my dollar from the boy. I'm sure he was surprised to have to actually pay up, but I was thirsty.

Although lizards in the house help keep

the bugs down, they can also add to the
overall mess level. Some of the lizards seem
to climb around on the rafters at night and
drop little poops the size and color of olive
pits with a white tip on the end. I haven't
actually caught them at it, but I think it must
be the geckos, which are larger than the anole
lizards. They only come out at night and hide
behind picture frames and in other strange
places during the day.

   A number of times after being away from
the house I have found decaying lizard
carcasses in the shower or under a chair.
Maybe they got trapped inside when we
locked up the house. Eventually the ants will
consume everything except the bones. The
strangest find I made was after some short-
term renters had put clear packing tape
around the edges of the windows thinking
that would help keep out the mosquitoes. It
looked tacky and I pulled off the tape when
I saw it, but it left a sticky residue around the
windows. Quite a bit later, when I was doing
some cleaning in that room, it looked like
some tiny sticks had gotten stuck along the
edge of the window. When I went to scrape
them off, I noticed that they were arranged
in a peculiar pattern. What really caught my

eye were the little ones together that looked like toes. Eventually I realized that the tiny sticks were lizard bones.

It must have gotten stuck in the glue from the tape and hung there by the side of the window until nothing was left but the little bones.

Outside, we have very occasionally seen bright green young iguanas prancing across the road, though the iguanas seem to prefer moister, flatter areas than our hillside. They are vegetarians and are mostly pretty shy, except there was a friendly one I petted once at the Maho Bay Camp. The grown up ones are darker and more ferocious looking, with a spiky crest down their backs and along their tails.

I thought everyone liked having the iguanas around, but Mr. Small, who comes to help us keep the termites from eating our wooden house, complained that the iguanas were displaced when the new cargo dock was being built and came rooting around in his yard. He is one of the few people I know who has a vegetable garden, and he said the iguanas had come in and eaten all his sweet potatoes and okra. I suggested that he put up a fence around his garden, but he said the iguanas can climb a fence, or dig under it, or climb a tree and drop down over into the garden, so it is hard to keep them away from tasty crops.

It seems likely that the iguanas came to the islands with ancestors of the Tainos, the native people who came up from South America. They seem too big to have come by themselves on rafts of debris like some of the smaller species. Probably they were brought along in the canoes as food, though most people these days would balk at the idea of roasting a lizard.

Bats

*B*ATS ARE REPORTED TO BE THE only surviving mammals that are native to these islands. The pre-Columbian Taino people often used figures of bats on their pottery, and seem to have associated them with the spirits of the dead which, like fruit bats, were thought to fly around at night feeding on guava. Besides fruit-eating bats, there are ones that eat only mosquitoes, and others that aren't so specialized in their appetites.

I haven't had much first-hand experience with Caribbean bats myself. Like the Taino, I tend to be fearful of going out alone at night, especially when there are dark creatures flying around. The closest I have gotten to a bat here was when I woke up one morning to

find a black one fluttering around in the toilet bowl. (At least I turned the light on before I went to sit down.) He was probably a roof bat, also known as a mastiff or dog-faced bat. They are mosquito eaters that commonly roost in the roofs of houses. They can crawl into tiny crevices under the metal roof, where it must be incredibly hot during the day. Supposedly they go into a torpor during the day and drop their body temperature to conserve energy. Maybe that helps them endure the heat. In the evening and early morning, they chase bugs, using clicks and squeaks we can't hear to bounce sound waves off the surfaces of objects to locate their prey.

Biologists have found that bats, birds and insects are regularly transported from one island to another during hurricanes and tropical storms. Instead of raining cats and dogs, it could be raining bats and bugs. I was doubtful about the effectiveness of that sort of airborne transit, but one clear morning after a night of thunder and lightning due to a passing tropical wave, I woke up to find a light layer of gray dust on the deck. A friend called and said she thought it was volcanic ash from Montserrat, which is only a few islands down on the chain of the Lesser

Antilles. Maybe it was mixed with the more common Sahara dust carried across the Atlantic on the trade winds. Soon we heard that the dome of the Soufriere Hills volcano on Montserrat had collapsed and the storm had picked up large quantities of the ash and deposited it on nearby islands. Later I saw a copy of Natural History magazine that happened to have an article on the travails of the bats on Montserrat. It said that in 1989, even before the volcano started acting up, Montserrat was blasted by Hurricane Hugo, which apparently blew many of the bats, along with the fruits and the trees, out across the ocean.

Biologists observed that in Montserrat the bats that roosted in caves survived the storm damage better than the ones that roosted in trees. Another factor was their willingness to eat a wide variety of foods – including flowers, insects and leaves – at a time when there weren't many fruits left. Surprisingly, one of the long-term impacts on those bats that survived was extensive dental decay and tooth loss. After the eruption, abrasive ash got into the bats' mouths when they ate fruits and groomed their fur, eroding the enamel on their teeth. So if you come across any bats with bad teeth, it's possible they could have been blown here from Montserrat.

Most people find bats a bit spooky, and probably wouldn't mind too much if they lost their teeth. Those teeth can be very intimidating, even though there are no vampire bats here and it is hard to imagine the fruit bats biting a person. My husband's grandmother said that bats could get stuck in your hair and bite you trying to get away, but I don't think she ever saw it happen. After I read that some bats will eat their weight in mosquitoes in one night, they started looking a lot more attractive to me. But it still seems like they have too many sharp teeth for just eating bugs and fruit. Many birds manage on a bug diet without any teeth at all.

Birds

WHEN WE FIRST ARRIVED WE PUT out sugar water in a bowl on the deck to attract the small bright yellow bananaquits that are common throughout the Caribbean. They are very cheery company, but once we had a cat around it didn't seem like a good idea to try to encourage birds to come onto the deck. They stay in the trees now, and build their nests in the spiny cactus tree in the yard, something no cat would want to climb.

The darker grassquits come onto the deck anyway, even without the lure of sugar. They often make their nests in the rafters under the roof over our deck. If the door is open they even will come into the house to look for nest-making material, and it is tough to chase them out again. They tend to fly up into the rafters and seem to forget where the door is.

Any food left outside catches the attention of the pearly-eyed thrashers, which are the most numerous and aggressive birds here. They especially like fruit, but seem to be willing to try anything. Once I even caught a 'thrashee' at the beach going after our lunch, poking a hole in a plastic bag to get a taste of the peanut butter and jelly sandwich inside.

The tiny green hummingbirds are beautifully iridescent as they hover around the flowers in the yard. They don't usually come into the house, but one day I heard a loud crack against one of the windows and when I went out to investigate I found two hummingbirds lying a few feet apart on the deck, knocked out. At first I thought they were dead, but when I got up close I could see that they were breathing faintly. Maybe they were chasing each other and didn't notice the glass. I kept checking on them and after about half an hour they got up and flew away again.

One summer we shared our deck with a family of gray kingbirds. I first noticed the parents when they were flying around carrying bits of nesting materials, including pieces of our mop, which had been left outside to dry. When I stood up on a chair to see where the nest was, I saw they were building it right in the corner of the gutter that collects rainwater off the roof and hooks up to the pipe carrying the water down into the cistern. While I was up there I could see one of the parents perched on the roof. When it saw me it flew straight at me, aiming at my eyes, to scare me off – quite successfully. Once the nest was finished, the parent birds hovered around making sure that none of us got near, which wasn't very likely since you would need a ladder to actually get up to the nest.

The kingbird is called a 'chichery' in the Virgin Islands, supposedly because of the constant loud 'cheery' sound it makes. I can tell you that it doesn't sound all that cheery at 4:30 in the morning, when they sometimes get up.

We could tell that the eggs had hatched when three little heads appeared over the edge of the gutter. Feeding time for the hatchlings often coincided with our own early dinner time on the deck, and it was quite a show. No one was more interested in the baby birds than our neighbor's black kitten, Mustafa, who was a frequent guest, especially at dinner time. Mustafa jumped straight up in the air to get a better look, then tried climbing up the screen to get at them, but he wasn't able to get close. I hadn't been very happy about having a bird's nest in our gutter, especially since there was precious little water in our cistern. I was also concerned that a big storm would wash the nest down the gutter so it would clog the drainpipe. But after watching Mustafa, I realized that the birds had picked a pretty good place for their nest – someplace safe from cats.

Bush Cats

WILD CATS ARE A MAJOR THREAT to the small wildlife on the island. Some of them start out as pets but later are abandoned, maybe when their owners move away. Abandoned cats have to figure out how to live off the land as best they can. Some have kittens that grow up in the wild, and then the feral cat population keeps on growing.

As soon as we moved into our original rental house there was an abandoned black and white cat that hung around looking for food. She was a sweet cat and we were happy for the company. My son called her Sylvester, after a favorite cartoon character, and we kept feeding her off and on for years since the house we bought was right next door.

Although sometimes we made sure she was fed by neighbors when we weren't around, lots of times she was on her own, living the 'bush cat' life. A number of other cats wandered in and out of our house as well, or lurked in the surrounding underbrush. There was a big, mean, one-eared tom cat that sometimes chased Sylvester, and sometimes stole food left out for friendlier cats. We never intentionally fed him, and he was definitely not pet material.

Ringtail was a different story altogether. She was a tiny kitten, pale and partly Siamese, who followed my older son home from a walk, crying loudly the whole way. Maybe she had been just recently abandoned, since she seemed so insistent on getting human attention. We fed her, but she seemed sickly, like she might have worms, and I said she had to stay outside. She was furious about being shut out and kept crying and scratching at the screens until I got up and dumped a pot of water on her to shut her up. The boys were outraged at my hard-heartedness, and later I found out that the real reason she finally quieted down was that they had brought her inside and let her cuddle with them in front of the TV. She was so affectionate that she would allow my younger son to wear her around his neck like a scarf, something our subsequent cats have never seemed to enjoy.

A few nights after Ringtail moved in, I was annoyed again when I woke up in the middle of the night and heard her racing around my sons' room knocking things over. When I got up to throw her out, I found that she was chasing down a big rat almost as large as she was. By the time I came in she had him down, but not dead, in the corner. Being an island mom by this time, I got the dustpan, scooped up the rat, picked up the cat, and threw them both out into the yard, while my sons slept on obliviously. I was more appreciative of Ringtail after that, since I felt she had contributed to protecting the family. When we left that summer, one of our neighbors adopted Ringtail and we were able to keep seeing her for a while until that neighbor moved away.

Although I don't feel badly about cats catching rats and mice, I am concerned about wild cats killing off the native birds and lizards. It's best if cats are kept inside as well-fed house pets, not out hunting for food, or just for sport. Promptly spaying or neutering any cats that come by is a good way to prevent increases in the numbers of unwanted, and underfed, animals on the island. And it's good for the birds and lizards, too.

Rats

AS FAR AS I CAN TELL, THERE ARE two kinds of rats here. The Norway rats (Rattus nevegius) are big, brown ugly ones who originally came over on the sailing ships and grew fat on sugar cane during the plantation days. Fruit rats are a type of black rat (Rattus rattus), also known as roof rats or tree rats. They are smaller and less nasty looking than the Norway rats and have white bellies. Besides fruit, they too apparently like sugar cane, although that is not as easy to find these days. Fruit rats often come into houses around the rafters, after climbing onto the roof from tree branches. Other than the rat Ringtail caught in my sons' bedroom, I think all of the rats I have seen around our house have been fruit rats.

One time when we arrived for the summer we noticed that something was getting into the bananas we left on the counter and taking bites out of them. I remembered that one of my neighbors had put her bananas in the oven to keep them safe from rats, so we tried that, which seemed to help. But then there were other invasions into the food in the cabinets. There were also some holes in the screens that we tried to fix without much success, so when Mr. Small came by to check for termites we asked him what we should do about rats in the pantry. He had some blue poison pellets he put on top of the cabinets, and we hoped things would quiet down after that.

That year Beanie Babies were everyone's favorite toy. They were small stuffed animals, maybe six inches long, filled with small beans. Children could cuddle with them, throw them across the room, juggle them, or compete to collect as many different ones as possible. Our boys weren't collectors, but we had brought down a few that tended to be thrown around the house. One morning my husband came upstairs for coffee, and was straightening up a pile of shoes and sports equipment in the corner when he jumped back and started shouting. He had reached down to pick up what he thought was a cute little Beanie Baby and at the last moment realized that instead it was a poisoned fruit rat. That wasn't a good way to start the day, but at least he didn't actually pick it up and throw it onto the couch. We felt badly about killing the poor little fruit rat, especially seeing it suffering. Most people have few qualms about killing rats though, particularly when they are getting into the food.

There are a variety of stories about the mongooses brought to the islands to kill the rats. Some people will remember a Rudyard Kipling story about a brave mongoose named Riki Tivi Tavi who killed a cobra, but few people have actually seen a mongoose before coming here, since they are native to India not the Americas. For the most part, the mongooses don't bother people, except that, like the thrashees, they will raid your picnic lunch if you leave it lying around at the beach. (I once saw one crawl entirely inside a paper bag and eat someone's sandwich while they were out snorkeling.) Otherwise you will see mongooses run across the road sometimes, and they seem relatively cute and unthreatening, despite the fact that they look a lot like weasels.

The first story most people hear is that the mongooses were brought to the islands to kill the rats that were eating the sugarcane, but the rats came out at night and the mongooses hunted by day, so it was an unsuccessful attempt to introduce biological pest control. Later I read that the mongooses did eat the Norway rats, having no trouble finding the sleeping rats in their nests. As a result, the number of fruit rats increased, maybe because mongooses couldn't climb trees, or because the competing Norway rats were gone, and/or because mongooses also ate the snakes, who would otherwise have also hunted down the fruit rats. Another story had it that the Norway rats learned to climb trees to get away from the mongooses. Maybe some mongooses learned to climb as well, because one person reported seeing a mongoose chase a rat up a tree. At least in some places, hungry mongooses became pests themselves, eating chickens, nesting wild birds, crabs, and iguanas as well as snakes and rats, and also spreading rabies. In any event, there don't seem to be any snakes here any more, but there are still some rats, and mongooses.

Frogs

IN THE EVENING A REMARKABLE crescendo of sound builds up around the house. In other parts of the world the night noises may come from crickets or cicadas. Here, much of the sound supposedly comes from tiny tree frogs. Occasionally I have seen a little frog on the outside stairs, yet it seems like there must be hundreds of them in every tree to make so much noise.

Just after dark the little coqui frogs start calling out to each other. During the day they hunt for insects and then in the evening they climb trees to avoid predators. In the morning they jump back down to the ground. Their scientific name is 'Eleuthero dactylus', which is Greek for 'free toes'. They are not web-footed, but have disks or pads on their toes to

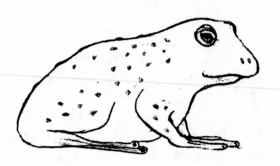

help them stick to slippery surfaces.

Both male and female coquis call loudly from holes and crevices in tree trunks or branches, declaring their presence and warning others to find their own shelter. The loudest sound, however, is the mating call of the male coqui frogs, which has a two-tone 'ko-kee' sound that can reach 100 decibels. They make the sound by moving air back and forth between their lungs and an expandable air sac below their mouths.

The male coqui frogs are loudest after a heavy rain, letting the females know that there is plenty of moisture and wet vegetation for successful breeding. During a mating embrace that can last up to 12 hours, the male fertilizes eggs as the female lays them in a damp place on the ground – usually inside a rolled-up leaf. Then the males will keep the eggs moist and guard them from predators for several weeks until they hatch. Unlike most frogs, the coquis don't lay eggs in the water or go through a tadpole stage. During the winter dry season, conditions are less favorable for mating and the frogs are generally quieter. Then they get moisture from condensed dew, or seek refuge in bromeliad plants or under damp leaves.

The other frogs of note are the non-native Cuban tree frogs that some years ago started invading the Virgin Islands. They may have originally been escapees from a lab experiment on St. Croix. These frogs are much bigger than the native ones and are voracious eaters. They reduce the natural biodiversity by consuming smaller frogs, plus baby birds, lizards and mice – whatever else they can fit into their big mouths.

The Cuban frogs are covered with toxic slime that can kill their predators. If you touch them, it can cause swelling, redness and itching on your skin or in your eyes. Although it is not clear how much effect the toxic frogs can have if they are in your drinking water, their appearance caused quite a stir when all of a sudden it seemed like there were toxic frogs in everyone's cistern. Or stacked up in the pipes leading from the gutters into the cistern.

Nobody wants slimy toxic frogs breeding in their drinking water, but it is not so easy to get them out. One Saturday I called a friend of mine and she said "I can't talk now. My husband is down in the cistern with his mask and snorkel and a net chasing frogs. When he gets one, he's throwing it up to me

to get rid of, so I have to go." I said okay, call
me back later. Just another day in paradise.

Termites

ONE OF OUR WILDEST TIMES WAS the night the termites flew up. The boys were still fairly young and we had just come down for a short trip, maybe for Thanksgiving vacation. During dinner there was a strong thunderstorm with heavy rain and lightning right out in the bay. The power went out for a while and then miraculously came back on again. We were just settling down after the storm, watching TV, when I noticed a few unusual bugs flying around the rafters upstairs. Within minutes there were hundreds of them in the house, then thousands, and then their wings started falling off and drifting down around us.

We abandoned the upstairs and ran downstairs where the doors and screens are tighter.

It seemed safe down there and my husband went to bed. I started reading to the boys until we began seeing some of the bugs flying around downstairs too. I went to check if the sliding glass doors were all tightly closed and saw that there were thousands of the bugs down along the bottom of the sliders crawling all over each other trying to squeeze in.

It felt like the night of the living dead, and we wondered how we would be able to fight off the would-be intruders in order to survive until morning. I got some heavy towels and jammed them into the spaces around the doors, but still some bugs were getting through. The boys got other towels and started whacking at the ones that got in and landed on the walls. They were getting in our hair and wings were flying everywhere as we raced around trying to clear the room. Eventually we were exhausted and things seemed to settle down pretty much. There was still a crawly mass of bugs outside the door, but most of the ones inside were on the ceiling and staying quiet so we finally turned off the lights and went to bed.

In the morning, there were bug bodies everywhere, and whenever we touched anything some wings would flutter up and then fall again. There were even bug bodies inside the frame of one of the paintings upstairs, behind the glass. We met some friends at the beach later that day and they said that it had happened at their house too. They said it was ground termites flying up because the heavy rain had flooded their nests. Everyone else seemed to know that the termites were attracted by the lights, and that they would stay outside if you turned off the lights right away. After that, whenever there was a sudden heavy rain, we would brace ourselves and get ready to turn out all the lights before another invasion could begin.

Later I learned that the story about the nests being flooded wasn't really true. The flying up is more of a planned dispersal so new nests can be formed. Termite colonies have several different types of members, including lots of workers (usually sterile females) who build nests, make trails and feed the others, a small number of soldiers (sterile males) to defend the nest and the workers out on the trails, and a few select males and females who get to do all the reproductive work. Once a year, a new group of potentially reproductive termite nymphs are generated, and these will develop wings so they can fly out of the nest, pair up, and create new colonies.

In the Caribbean, the termites usually fly up after the first heavy rain in the fall. Like the frogs, they seem to prefer their nesting sites to be moist. The lucky ones pair off, drop their flimsy wings and begin mating. Usually only a few are successful. The ones that, like so many bugs, are irrepressibly attracted to the bright lights inside your house, generally will not get lucky. They will not usually find what they need to nest, even if they do explore the inside of your picture frames, and will instead dry up and die, after littering the place with wings.

There seem to be two kinds of termites here: the ones that nest under the ground and the ones that make the big interesting nests in trees. Both kinds can eat your house, or any part of it made out of wood, unless the wood is pressure treated with an arsenic-based poison, or is from a type of tree that termites don't care for. And it seems that both types of termites start new colonies through dispersal flights, not just the smaller ground termites.

When we first rented the house in Fish

Bay, I noticed strange markings across the concrete floor downstairs that would not sweep up. I didn't pay much attention to them at the time. Later, in the wooden house we bought, I learned that those were the beginnings of termite trails. Somehow a termite search party from a nest in a tree hundreds of feet away was able to determine that the new baseboard in the downstairs bathroom was made out of untreated wood. They hollowed it out from the inside until there was nothing but a thin veneer you could stick your finger through, with some scraps of dust behind it.

People complain about termites getting in and eating their furniture, books, papers, and stuff stored in cardboard boxes. This is definitely not a good place to be a pack rat. But the termites are actually doing an important job by cleaning up all the old dead wood and recycling debris. They don't usually harm living trees, even the ones their nests are on, and they help prevent forest fires. They are regular little girl scouts, really.

Ants

*E*VEN IF YOU SEALED UP EVERY crack in the house, the ants would still find a way to get in. The ones in the house don't generally bite though, so they are more welcome than invading mosquitoes, and even better recyclers than the termites. They can help with the housework by disposing of the dead moths and the crumbs that collect under the couch.

There are biting ants – fire ants – but they mostly stay in the yard, joining forces with the stinging nettles and snake cactus to let you know your efforts at gardening are not welcome.

The ants inside the house are very small and non-threatening. There are just a lot of them. I have heard that if you gathered up all the ants in the world they would outweigh the more than 6 billion people currently on the earth.

The ants will find any scrap of food left out on the counter, in the cat's dish or in an unsecured garbage bag. The smallest ones can even sneak into a sealed package of food in the cupboard or crawl into a jar along the ridges of a screw-top cap. It is amazing to me how quickly the ants will swarm over the smallest drop of milk on the table or crumb on the counter. They seem to have an incredibly effective communication system. The ones out scouting for food leave a chemical trail of pheromones to show the others where to go and when you turn your back a busy chain of ants starts streaming across the kitchen.

If you have any doubts about whether ants can get into something, it is best to keep it in the refrigerator. Most ants can't survive in the cold. They prefer warm, humid environments. My husband didn't think that peanut butter belonged in the refrigerator since his mother in Minnesota kept it out, so he left it on the counter and soon found out how much ants enjoy sugary, fatty foods. My younger son was still small and insisted that he didn't mind ants in his peanut butter and jelly sandwiches – they just added some extra protein. Certainly it would not have been easy to pick them all out.

When the ants get into the breakfast cereal, I just put the box into the freezer. That kills the ants, although they are still there and float to the top when you add milk. My son now complains when he finds them, saying they have a bitter taste.

The most common ants here seem to be Pharaoh ants. They got their name because they were mistakenly believed to be one of the Biblical plagues visited on Egypt to persuade the Pharaoh to let the Israelites go. (I think there were locusts, flies and lice.) They do come from Africa and probably came over on the sailing ships. Pharaoh ants make their nests in the house and there may be many thousands in one colony. If you spray them, they will split up into several colonies and spread out into other parts of the house.

Ants have a social organization similar to that of termites, though there may be more than one queen in a nest. The sterile females do all the work, finding and gathering the food, as well as caring for the young and protecting the nest. The males only live long enough to mate with the queen. The Pharaoh ants do produce reproductive youths with wings, but they don't actually fly up. They do their mating in the nest.

There are also Thief ants that are even smaller than the Pharaoh ants. They sometimes make tiny tunnels into the larger ants' nests and steal the eggs and larvae. These ants are more likely to have their nests outside, just coming in sometimes.

Their reproductive youths actually do fly up to find mates, but they are too small to be scary.

There seem to be seasonal variations in ant immigration, and a variety of triggers for asylum-seeking. Sometimes people say there are more ants in the house because it is too dry outside and they are looking for moisture. Other times they say it is too wet and the ants are coming in (walking, not flying) because their nests in the ground are getting flooded.

Soapy water is one of the best solutions for ant invasions because it washes away the chemical trails laid down by the worker ants. Washing dishes right away also keeps the ants from congregating in the kitchen and encourages them to take the party somewhere else – like outside. I have read that putting cloves or sage around the windows and doors will keep ants from walking in. And cayenne pepper is supposed to burn their feet. They also can't walk across water, so we were advised to set the cat's dish inside a larger plate of water. Some ants still got over the moat. Maybe they formed living bridges.

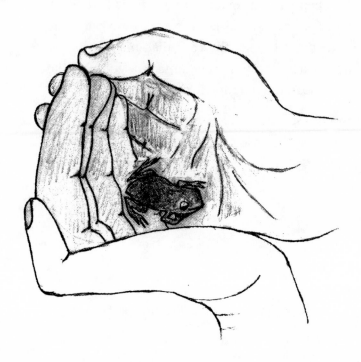

Partners in Paradise

MY YOUNGER SON THINKS that the world would be a better place if all the mosquitoes were dead. Certainly many millions of people have died due to diseases carried by mosquitoes, but so far he has only been annoyed and harassed, and has little to complain about really. However, if he feels strongly enough about it, maybe instead of declaring a unilateral war on mosquitoes, he should team up with the scorpions, lizards, spiders, bats and birds and help them so they can eat more of the mosquitoes hanging around the house.

In my current environmental work for the United Nations, one of the key strategies is to try to build 'partnerships for sustainable development.' Generally, these are partnerships between governments, private companies and citizens action groups. Unfortunately, non-human societal groups are not yet recognized at the UN.

Still, I think there are great unexplored possibilities for inter-species cooperation. I particularly like the way the ants and birds and fruit rats help me dispose of organic garbage like banana peels and apple cores so they don't have to be packed up and shipped to the landfill in St. Thomas. I really think we have some environmental and political interests in common.

I know some people will say "Aren't we better than bugs? And rodents and amphibians? Why should we cooperate with them? Let's just kill them off." Most religions do not view these creatures as having souls to be saved. More often, they are seen as agents for the devil. Buddhists, however, take a longer view, and see the worth in even seemingly lowly forms of life. Personally, I think it is probably a good idea to be respectful of other living creatures, even if you don't believe in reincarnation and are not concerned that poor choices might mean you will spend your next life in an ant colony.

In any event, it seems wise to first try to

understand what the creatures around us are doing. We can always try to kill them later. Some of them are quite fascinating and maybe we can learn a few things from them about sustainability.

I haven't gotten to the point yet where I prefer the company of lizards and spiders to people, despite the fact that some days they seem easier to understand. I do feel that we have a responsibility to them, however, especially since they were here first. At least we shouldn't wipe them all out, intentionally or unintentionally, without anyone thinking through the consequences or even noticing what is happening.

Printed in the United States
75082LV00002B/2